Salt Dough
F · U · N
PETRA BOASE

ACROPOLIS
BOOKS

First published in 1996 by Lorenz Books

Lorenz Books is an imprint of Anness Publishing Limited
Boundary Row Studios
1 Boundary Row
London SE1 8HP

© Anness Publishing Limited

Distributed in Canada by Raincoast Books Distribution Limited

ISBN 1 85967 220 5

A CIP catalogue record is available from the British Library.

Publisher: Joanna Lorenz
Senior Children's Editor: Caroline Beattie
Photography: John Freeman
Design: Tony Sambrook

Printed and bound by Star Standard, Singapore.

Introduction

Salt dough is easy to make and fun to do. Before you start work on the exciting projects in this book, make sure you have all your tools by you and the surface you are working on is clean. After you have finished your salt dough project ask an adult to put it in the oven and to take it out for you when it is ready. Allow the salt dough to cool thoroughly before you start painting. If you don't use all the salt dough you have made store it in an airtight container or a plastic bag and put it in the fridge. When you come to use it again, knead it well with a sprinkling of flour. The projects in this book all make wonderful presents, but remember that salt dough is fragile, so handle it with care. Have fun!

Petra Boase

Contents

GETTING STARTED

SALT DOUGH FUN

Materials & Equipment

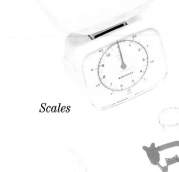

Scales

Pastry cutters

Measuring jug

Scissors

Water   *Salt*

ACRYLIC PAINT
This paint gives a smooth finish and is easy to apply. If you don't have exactly the colour you want, mix paints together to make new colours.

BAKING TRAY
This is used to put the salt dough on while it is cooking in the oven.

COCKTAIL STICKS
These are useful for making holes and patterns in the salt dough before it is baked in the oven.

COOLING RACK
After the salt dough has baked in the oven, place it on a cooling rack to cool before painting.

FLOUR
One of the main ingredients for making salt dough. It is also sprinkled on a flat surface before rolling out salt dough so that it doesn't stick.

FOOD COLOURING
This is used to colour salt dough while it is still raw.

KNIFE
You'll need a knife for cutting out salt dough and for cutting round templates. Knives are sharp so be very careful and ask for help.

MEASURING JUG
This is a jug with measurements marked up the side and is used for measuring the exact amount of water for the salt dough recipe.

MODELLING TOOL
This is used for cutting the salt dough as well as modelling it into interesting shapes.

OVEN GLOVES
These must always be worn when removing a baking tray from the oven and when handling salt dough that you have just baked.

PAINTBRUSHES
These come in an assortment of different sizes and thicknesses and are used for painting and varnishing the salt dough. They are also used for glueing and must always be washed after use.

PALETTE KNIFE
This is a wide flat knife used for lifting raw salt dough onto a baking tray and for placing it onto a cooling rack when it has baked.

PARCHMENT PAPER
This prevents the salt dough sticking to the baking tray when it is baking.

PASTRY CUTTERS
These are either metal or plastic and come in a wide range of shapes and sizes. They are used to cut out shapes from the salt dough.

OIL
One of the main ingredients for making salt dough. It is also used to grease moulds to prevent the salt dough sticking to them.

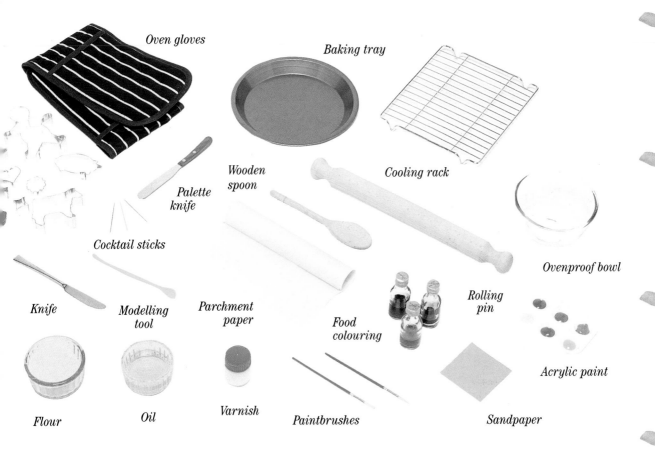

Oven gloves

Baking tray

Cooling rack

Wooden spoon

Palette knife

Cocktail sticks

Ovenproof bowl

Knife

Modelling tool

Parchment paper

Food colouring

Rolling pin

Acrylic paint

Flour

Oil

Varnish

Paintbrushes

Sandpaper

OVENPROOF BOWL
This is used for making salt dough in. It is also used as a mould for making a salt dough bowl.

ROLLING PIN
This is used for rolling a piece of salt dough flat. Dust the rolling pin with flour first as this will stop it from sticking to the dough.

SALT
One of the main ingredients for making salt dough.

SANDPAPER
Before the baked salt dough is painted, the surface needs to be smoothed, which is done by gently rubbing a piece of sandpaper over it.

SCALES
These are used to measure the ingredients for the salt dough.

SCISSORS
These are used to cut an assortment of materials. They should not be too sharp and must be handled carefully at all times.

VARNISH
This is applied over the paint to protect it and give it a shiny finish.

WATER
One of the main ingredients for making salt dough. It is also used to help stick raw pieces of salt dough to each other.

WOODEN SPOON
This is used to mix all the raw ingredients of salt dough together.

How to Make Salt Dough

YOU WILL NEED

2½ C. *300 g (11 oz) flour*
¾ C. *300 g (11 oz) salt*
200 ml (7 fl oz) water
30 ml (2 tbsp) vegetable oil

① Measure the flour and the salt and put them in a large bowl together. Mix them up well.

② Measure 200 ml (7 fl oz) of water in a measuring jug. Gradually pour the water over the flour and salt and mix well.

③ Pour 30 ml (2 tablespoonfuls) of vegetable oil over the mixture and mix it in well (*left*).

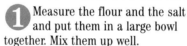

④ Take the salt dough out of the bowl and place it on a clean surface that has been sprinkled with flour. Knead the dough until it is firm and wrap it in clear film or put it in a plastic bag. Place the dough in the fridge for half an hour before you use it (*right*).

Decorating & Cutting

1 To colour salt dough, roll some salt dough into a ball. Make a small well in the centre of it, then carefully pour in a few drops of food colouring.

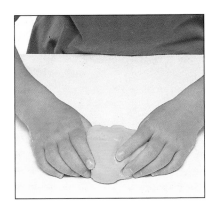

2 Knead the colouring into the salt dough on a flour-dusted surface until the colour of the dough is even. Add more food colouring if you need to.

3 Before you roll out salt dough, always make sure that the surface you are working on is well dusted with flour. If you don't have a rolling pin, use a smooth bottle.

4 Pastry cutters come in plenty of different shapes and sizes. When you have cut out your shapes from the dough, always save the leftovers to use again (*left*).

5 Sometimes you will want to decorate your salt dough projects with patterns. There are all sorts of tools you can use and each one can create a different kind of pattern on the dough (*right*).

Tracing a Template

1 If you need to, enlarge the template using a photocopier. Place a piece of tracing paper over the template and draw around the shape using a soft, blunt pencil.

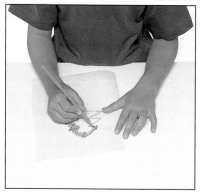

2 Take the tracing paper off the template and turn it over. Rub over the back of the traced image with a soft pencil.

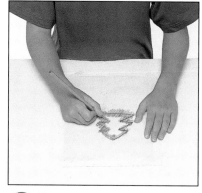

3 Place the tracing on a piece of card or paper with the rubbed pencil side facing down. Draw over the shape with the pencil to transfer the picture. Press hard.

4 Carefully cut out the shape in paper or card around the line you have transferred.

Finishing Off

1 To bake salt dough, first cover a baking tray with parchment paper. This prevents the salt dough sticking to the tray. For flat pieces of dough, use a palette knife to lift the salt dough gently onto the tray. Leave it in the oven to bake. (If you don't have access to an oven you can leave the salt dough to harden at room temperature. This will take several days.)

2 When the salt dough has baked, carefully place it on a cooling rack to cool.

3 When the salt dough has cooked, you may notice that it is a bit rough. To smooth it down, use a piece of sandpaper. Be gentle, as salt dough is very fragile.

4 You can then use acrylic paints to paint the salt dough. If you are using lots of different colours, let each colour dry before you paint the next colour.

5 When the paint has thoroughly dried, varnish over the paint using a craft varnish which gives a nice shiny finish.

SAFETY FIRST!

ALWAYS ask an adult to help you light the oven or to set the oven temperature. And always ask an adult to help you put the salt dough into the oven to bake and take it out of the oven when it has finished baking. Make sure they wear a pair of oven gloves.

Fish Card

This special card will make someone very happy and it can be hung anywhere round the home.

YOU WILL NEED

Salt dough
Rolling pin
Knife
Thick card
Parchment paper
Baking tray
Cooling rack
Oven gloves
Sandpaper
Acrylic paint
Paintbrush
Varnish
Card glue
Hole punch
Ribbon

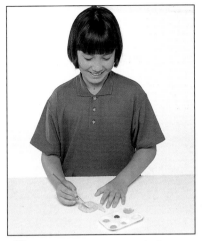

1 Roll out a piece of salt dough to approximately 1 cm thick and cut out an enlarged shape of a fish using the template on page 10.

2 Decorate the fish with small balls of salt dough and different marks. Place it on a piece of parchment paper on a baking tray and leave it in the oven for about six hours at 120°C/250°F/Gas ½.

3 When the fish has cooked, remove it from the oven with a pair of oven gloves and allow it to cool. Gently smooth the surface with a piece of sandpaper and paint it with bright colours.

4 When the paint has dried, varnish the fish and glue it onto a colourful piece of card. Punch a hole at the top of the card with a hole punch and tie a piece of ribbon through it into a bow.

Zigzag Letter Rack

This is the perfect way of storing your letters and pieces of stationery so that you don't lose them. Don't use it as a toast rack!

YOU WILL NEED

Salt dough
Rolling pin
Ruler
Knife
Parchment paper
Baking tray
Oven gloves
Cooling rack
Sandpaper
Acrylic paint
Varnish
Paintbrush

1 Roll out a piece of salt dough to about 1.5 cm thick. For the base of the rack, measure a rectangular piece 12 cm by 8 cm, cut it out and place it on a piece of parchment paper on a baking tray.

2 For the dividing walls of the rack, measure and cut out two pieces each measuring 8 cm by 5 cm and cut a zigzag edge along one of the long sides. Cut another piece measuring 8 cm by 6 cm and cut a spiky zigzag edge along one of the long sides. Place the shapes on the baking tray with the base and put them in the oven to bake for about three hours at 120°C/250°F/Gas½.

3 Remove the baking tray from the oven with a pair of oven gloves and place the shapes on a cooling rack. When the shapes have cooled, join the two shorter walls to each end of the base with wet salt dough and join the taller wall in between the two. Place the letter rack back on the baking tray and put it in the oven to harden for another three hours.

4 When the letter rack has cooled, smooth the edges with a piece of sandpaper, then paint and varnish it.

Wiggly Snake Frame

This fun frame could be used for a mirror or a picture.

YOU WILL NEED

Salt dough
Modelling tool
Parchment paper
Baking tray
Cooling rack
Oven gloves
Sandpaper
Paintbrush
Acrylic paint
Varnish
Felt
Scissors
Glue
Picture frame

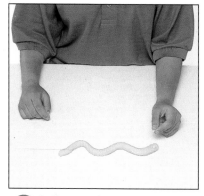

1 Roll out a piece of salt dough into a long roll. Bend it into a wiggly shape. Roll two small balls of salt dough for the eyes and attach them onto one end of the snake. Make three more snakes in the same way.

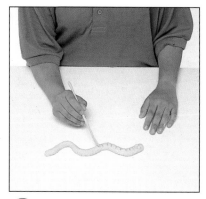

2 Decorate each snake with a different pattern, eg spots and stripes, using the modelling tool. Place the snakes on a piece of parchment paper on a baking tray and bake them for about four hours at 120°C/250°F/Gas ½.

3 When the snakes have hardened, remove them from the oven with a pair of oven gloves and place them on a cooling rack. When the snakes are cool enough, sand them down, then paint and varnish them.

4 For the tongue of each snake, cut out a piece of coloured felt and glue it under the snake's head.

5 Paint the frame using two colours to make a chequerboard pattern. Then glue the snakes on, one on each edge of the frame.

Gold Star Badge

Reward yourself or your friends with this glittering star badge. You could also make it using different colours.

1 Trace and enlarge the large star on page 10 to make the template. Roll out a piece of salt dough to about 1 cm thick and place the template on the dough. Cut around the template. Place the star on a piece of parchment paper on a baking tray and leave it in the oven for about four hours at 120°C/250°F/ Gas ½.

2 Remove the baking tray from the oven with a pair of oven gloves and place the star on a cooling rack. When the star has cooled, gently smooth any rough edges with a piece of sandpaper and paint the star gold.

YOU WILL NEED

Salt dough	Sandpaper
Rolling pin	Gold paint
Knife	Paintbrush
Parchment paper	Glitter
Baking tray	Gemstones
Cooling rack	Glue
Oven gloves	Badge pin

3 When the paint has dried, glue on a mixture of sequins, gemstones and glitter.

4 Glue the badge pin onto the back of the star. Leave the glue to harden before trying on the badge.

Cows on a Box

Recycle an old shoe box or a chocolate box by painting it and decorating it with salt dough shapes. The cows have been glued onto a box that was painted to look like a meadow.

YOU WILL NEED

Salt dough
Rolling pin
Animal pastry cutters
Parchment paper
Baking tray
Oven gloves
Cooling rack
Sandpaper
Acrylic paint
Paintbrush
Varnish
Card box
Glue

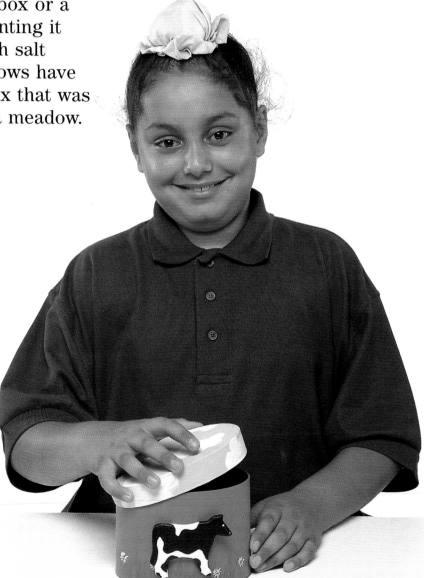

1 Roll out a piece of salt dough to approximately 1 cm thick. Using an animal pastry cutter, cut out salt dough shapes. Place the shapes on a piece of parchment paper on a baking tray and place them in the oven to bake for about five hours at 120°C/250°F/Gas ½.

2 When the shapes have hardened, remove the baking tray from the oven wearing a pair of oven gloves. When they have cooled down, smooth the edges with a piece of sandpaper. Paint the animals and leave them to dry, then apply a coat of varnish.

3 Paint the outside of the box green for the grass, then decorate it with small daisies. Paint the lid of the box blue for the sky, and add fluffy white clouds. Leave the paint to dry thoroughly.

4 Glue the animal shapes onto the outside of the painted box.

Beautiful Beads

This colourful necklace will jazz up a plain T-shirt.

YOU WILL NEED

Salt dough
Garden stick or skewer
Parchment paper
Baking tray
Cooling rack
Oven gloves
Acrylic paints
Paintbrush
Varnish
Coloured cord or ribbon

1 To make the round beads, roll small pieces of salt dough in the palm of your hand. For the flat beads, roll them first then pat them down on a flat surface.

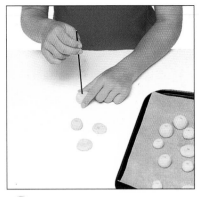

2 Make a hole through the centre of each bead with a garden stick or a skewer. Place the beads on a piece of parchment paper on a baking tray and bake them in the oven for about four hours at 120°C/250°F/Gas ½.

3 When the beads are hard, remove the tray from the oven using a pair of oven gloves and leave them to cool on a cooling rack. Paint the beads with bright-coloured paints. When the paint has dried apply a coat of varnish.

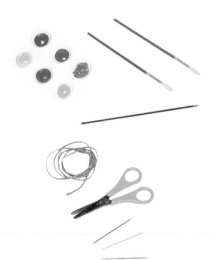

4 When the varnish has dried, thread the beads onto a piece of coloured cord and tie the two ends of the cord in a knot to fit around your neck.

Family of Pigs

Why not make lots of different families of animals (cows or sheep, for example) so that you begin to make a mini farm?

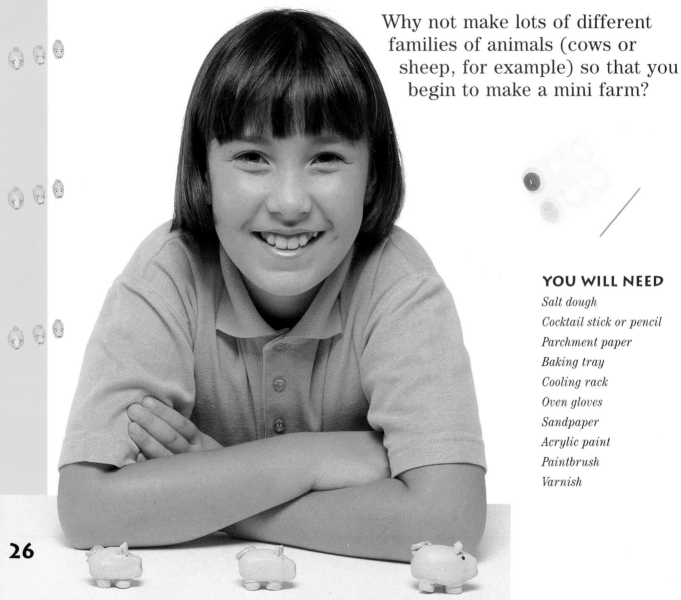

YOU WILL NEED

Salt dough

Cocktail stick or pencil

Parchment paper

Baking tray

Cooling rack

Oven gloves

Sandpaper

Acrylic paint

Paintbrush

Varnish

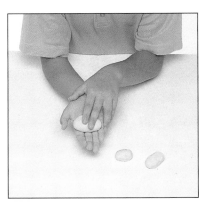

1 For each pig, roll a different-sized piece of salt dough in the palm of your hand to make an oval shape. Gently shape one end into a pig's face. Attach two small triangles of dough onto each pig's head for the ears. Mark the eyes and the nostrils with the tip of a pencil or with a cocktail stick.

2 Roll a small piece of salt dough into a long strip for each pig's tail and stick one onto the back of each pig with a dab of water in a coil shape. Place the pigs on a piece of parchment paper on a baking tray.

3 Make the legs from small balls of salt dough. Bake them in the oven with the pig bodies, for about five hours at 120°C/250°F/Gas ½.

4 When the pigs and the legs have hardened, remove them from the oven with a pair of oven gloves and place them on a cooling rack. When they have cooled, join four legs onto each pig's body with a piece of salt dough and a dab of water and place them back in the oven at the same temperature to harden together for two hours (*left*).

5 When the pigs have cooled, smooth any rough parts with a piece of sandpaper and then paint and varnish them (*right*).

Christmas Tree Decorations

Decorate your Christmas tree and home with these fun decorations. If you have a pet dog, don't hang them at the bottom of the tree as it may think they are dog biscuits!

YOU WILL NEED

Salt dough
Rolling pin
Knife
Parchment paper
Baking tray
Garden stick
Cooling rack
Oven gloves
Sandpaper
Acrylic paint
Paintbrush
Glue
Sequins
Glitter or glitter glue
Ribbon

28

1 Trace and enlarge the snowman and the Christmas tree on page 10 to make the templates. Roll out a piece of salt dough to about 1 cm thick and cut out the shapes using the templates. Place the shapes on a piece of parchment paper on a baking tray.

2 Make a hole at the top of each shape with a garden stick. For the snowman's nose stick on a small piece of dough in the shape of a carrot with a dab of water. Place them in the oven for about six hours at 120°C/250°F/Gas $\frac{1}{2}$.

3 When the shapes have cooled, smooth the edges with a piece of sandpaper. Paint the snowman white and paint on a scarf, his face, his arms and some buttons.

  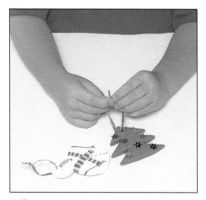

4 Paint the Christmas tree green and decorate it with sequins and glitter or glitter glue.

5 Tie a piece of ribbon through the hole of each shape and tie them onto the Christmas tree.

Coiled Plate

This plate is for decoration only! Remember to use an ovenproof plate for the mould.

YOU WILL NEED

Salt dough
Food colouring
Ovenproof plate
Vegetable oil
Oven gloves
Cooling rack
Sandpaper
Paintbrush
Varnish

1 You will need three different food colourings and three medium-sized balls of salt dough. Make a small well in the centre of one salt dough ball and pour in a few drops of food colouring. Knead the salt dough well on a flour-dusted surface until it has been completely coloured. Colour the other two balls of salt dough in the same way.

2 Rub a few drops of vegetable oil over the ovenproof plate to prevent the salt dough from sticking when it is baking. Roll the first coloured ball of salt dough into a long roll and, starting in the middle of the plate, coil it round. Roll another coloured piece of salt dough into a roll and join it to the end of the first piece. Continue until you have completely covered the plate.

3 Decorate the edge of the plate with small coloured dots of salt dough and the middle of the plate with one spot. Bake the plate in the oven for about six hours at 120°C/ 250°F/Gas ½.

4 When the plate has baked, allow it to cool and then smooth down the edges with a piece of sandpaper. Finally paint on a coat of varnish.

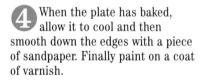

Earrings with Gems

You don't even have to have pierced ears to wear these eye-catching earrings as they just clip onto your ear lobes.

YOU WILL NEED

Salt dough
Modelling tool
Parchment paper
Baking tray
Oven gloves
Cooling rack
Sandpaper
Acrylic paint
Paintbrush
Gemstones or sequins
Glue
*Clip-on earring
    attachments*

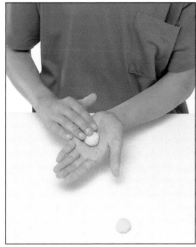

1 For each earring, roll a small piece of salt dough in the palm of your hand into a ball about the size of a cherry.

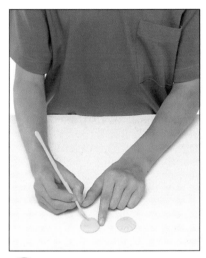

2 Gently flatten the ball between your fingers and mark the edge of each shape with a modelling tool as shown. Place the earrings on a piece of parchment paper on a baking tray and leave them in the oven for about four hours at 120°C/250°F/Gas ½.

3 When the earrings have hardened, place them on a cooling rack to cool down. Smooth down any rough edges with a piece of sandpaper. Paint each earring, then glue a sequin or gemstone in the centre of each one.

4 When the paint and glue have dried, turn the earrings over and glue on the earring attachments. Leave the glue to harden before trying the earrings on.

Square Container

This container is made by part-baking the five pieces then joining them together with wet salt dough and baking them again to harden into one piece.

YOU WILL NEED

Salt dough
Ruler
Knife
Parchment paper
Baking tray
Oven gloves
Cooling rack
Sandpaper
Acrylic paint
Paintbrush
Varnish

1 Roll out a piece of salt dough to about 1.5 cm thick. Measure a square 10 cm by 10 cm for the base of the container on the salt dough, and cut it out.

2 Measure four pieces 10 cm by 2.5 cm for the sides of the container and cut them out. Place all the pieces on a piece of parchment paper on a baking tray and put them in the oven to bake for three hours at 120°C/250°F/Gas ½.

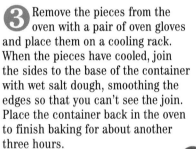

3 Remove the pieces from the oven with a pair of oven gloves and place them on a cooling rack. When the pieces have cooled, join the sides to the base of the container with wet salt dough, smoothing the edges so that you can't see the join. Place the container back in the oven to finish baking for about another three hours.

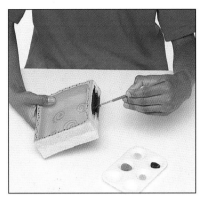

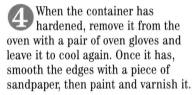

4 When the container has hardened, remove it from the oven with a pair of oven gloves and leave it to cool again. Once it has, smooth the edges with a piece of sandpaper, then paint and varnish it.

Strawberry Flowerpot

Give an ordinary plant pot a face-lift by turning it into this smart container.

YOU WILL NEED

Salt dough
Rolling pin
Knife
Modelling tool
Parchment paper
Baking tray
Oven gloves
Cooling rack
Sandpaper
Acrylic paint
Paintbrush
Varnish
Terracotta flowerpot
Strong glue

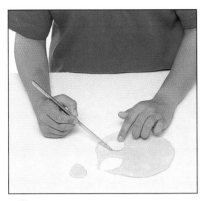

1 Trace the strawberry on page 11 to make the template. Roll out a piece of salt dough to about 1.5 cm thick and place the template on the dough. Cut round the template several times.

2 Using the modelling tool, mould small salt dough leaves and attach them to the top of each strawberry with a dab of water. Place the strawberries on a piece of parchment paper on a baking tray and put them in the oven to bake for about four hours at 120°C/ 250°F/Gas ½.

3 When the strawberries have hardened, remove the baking tray from the oven with a pair of oven gloves and place them on a cooling rack to cool. When they have cooled, smooth the edges with a piece of sandpaper and paint and varnish the strawberries.

4 Paint the terracotta flowerpot. When the paint has dried glue the strawberries round the rim.

Heart & Star Rings

These rings are great fun. You can make them in all sorts of different shapes and sizes. Remember to take them off before you have a bath!

YOU WILL NEED

Salt dough
Rolling pin
Knife
Parchment paper
Baking tray
Cooling rack
Oven gloves
Sandpaper
Acrylic paints
Paintbrush
Varnish
Metal ring attachment
Strong glue

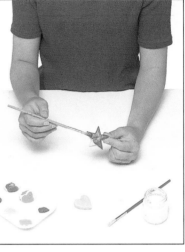

1 Trace the small heart and star on page 11 to make the templates. Roll out a piece of salt dough to approximately 1 cm thick and place the templates on the dough. Cut around the templates with the knife. Place the shapes on a piece of parchment paper on a baking tray and bake them in the oven for about four hours at 120°C/250°F/Gas½.

2 When the shapes have hardened remove the tray from the oven (using a pair of oven gloves) and transfer them to a cooling rack. Once they have cooled down, smooth any rough edges with sandpaper.

3 Now you can paint them in bright colours. When the paint has dried, apply a coat of varnish and leave it to dry.

4 Glue a ring attachment onto the back of each shape and leave the glue to dry before trying on the rings.

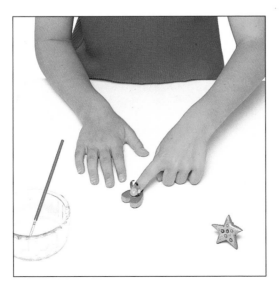

Space Rocket Door Plaque

Decorate your bedroom door with this futuristic space rocket. Why not make different ones for other rooms in your home?

YOU WILL NEED

Salt dough
Rolling pin
Knife
Garden stick
Parchment paper
Baking tray
Cooling rack
Oven gloves
Sandpaper
Acrylic paint
Paintbrush
Varnish

1 Trace the rocket on page 11 to make the template. Roll out a piece of salt dough to approximately 1 cm thick. Lay the template on the dough and cut round it.

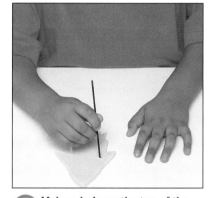

2 Make a hole on the top of the rocket with a garden stick, then mark out the areas of the rocket by gently pressing the stick into the dough. Place the rocket on a piece of parchment paper on a baking tray and bake for about seven hours at 120°C/250°F/Gas ½.

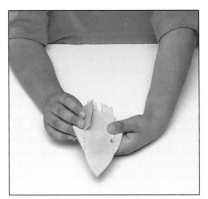

3 When the dough has hardened, remove the rocket from the oven with a pair of oven gloves. When it has cooled down, smooth the edges of the rocket with a piece of sandpaper.

4 Paint the rocket and add your name. When the paint has dried, varnish the rocket and hang it on your bedroom door or wall.

Pinch Pots

You do not need a mould for these pots; you can just shape them with your hands. Make a collection of them in different sizes as they are very useful for keeping bits and pieces in or just for decoration.

YOU WILL NEED

Salt dough
Parchment paper
Baking tray
Oven gloves
Cooling rack
Sandpaper
Acrylic paint
Paintbrush
Varnish

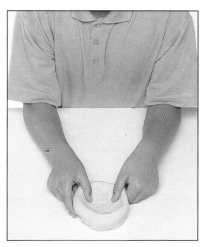

1 Roll a piece of salt dough in the palm of your hand into a ball for each bowl.

2 Use your thumbs to make a dip in the centre of the salt dough ball and shape it into a bowl, gradually pinching it out.

3 Decorate the top edge of each bowl with small balls of salt dough, sticking them on with a dab of water. Carefully place the bowls on a piece of parchment paper on a baking tray and put them in the oven to bake for about six hours at 120°C/250°F/Gas ½.

4 When the bowls have cooled, smooth any rough patches with a piece of sandpaper and paint them different colours. When the paint has dried, apply a coat of varnish.

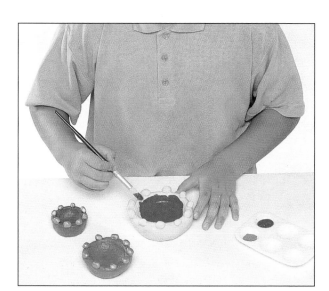

43

Flower Frame

This bright and cheerful frame will add colour to any shelf or wall. You could even paint the flowers to match the colour of your room.

YOU WILL NEED

Salt dough

Rolling pin

Knife

Parchment paper

Baking tray

Round pastry cutter

Cooling rack

Oven gloves

Sandpaper

Acrylic paint

Paintbrush

Varnish

Picture frame

Glue

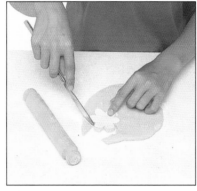

1 Trace the flower on page 11 to make the template. Roll out a piece of salt dough about 1 cm thick. Place the template on the dough and cut round it several times.

2 Place the flowers on a piece of parchment paper on a baking tray. Using a small round pastry cutter, cut out a round shape of salt dough for the centre of each flower and attach it to the flower with a dab of water. Bake the flowers in the oven for about five hours at 120°C/250°F/Gas ½.

3 When the flowers have hardened, remove the baking tray from the oven with a pair of oven gloves. Place the flowers on a cooling rack and when they have cooled smooth the edges with a piece of sandpaper. Paint the flowers in lots of bright colours. When the paint has dried varnish them.

4 Paint the picture frame if you need to, in a colour that goes with the flowers. Arrange the flowers on the frame, and glue them on.

45

Age Badge

Show off your age by wearing one of these fun badges.
You could make them for your friends on their birthdays, too.

YOU WILL NEED

Salt dough

Rolling pin

Knife

Garden stick or pencil

Parchment paper

Baking tray

Cooling rack

Oven gloves

Sandpaper

Acrylic paint

Paintbrush

Varnish

Badge pin

Glue

1 Trace the crown on page 11 to make the template. Roll out a piece of salt dough to about 1 cm thick then place the template on the dough and cut round it.

2 Decorate the points of the crown with small balls of dough. Roll a piece of salt dough into a long strip and stick it onto the crown with a dab of water, in the shape of your age. Decorate the points of the crown and the number with a stick or a pencil. Place the crown on a piece of parchment paper on a baking tray and put it in the oven to bake for about five hours at 120°C/250°F/Gas ½.

3 When the crown has cooled, smooth the edges with a piece of sandpaper. Paint the crown and then varnish it.

4 Glue a badge pin onto the back of the crown and leave the glue to harden before trying on the badge.

6

7

8

9

10

47

Heart Pendant

Your friends will be very envious when they see you wearing this beautiful pendant, and it's so easy to make!

YOU WILL NEED

Salt dough
Rolling pin
Knife
Garden stick or skewer
Parchment paper
Baking tray
Cooling rack
Oven gloves
Sandpaper
Acrylic paint
Paintbrush
Sequins
Gemstones
Glitter
Glue
Ribbon or cord

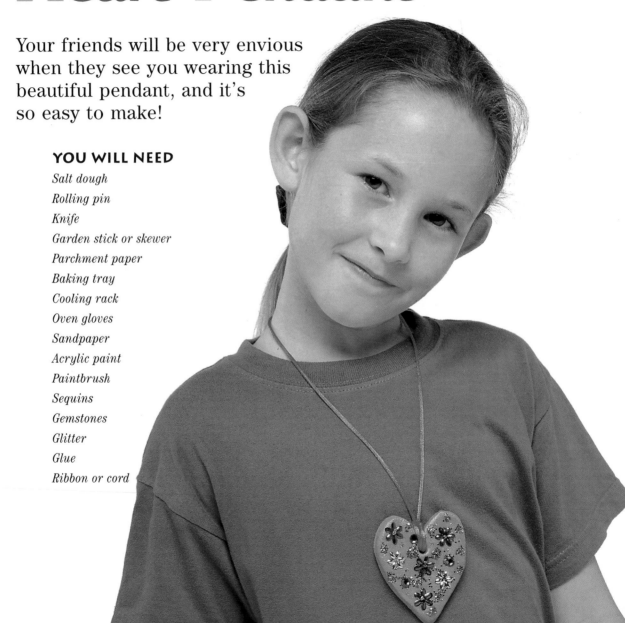

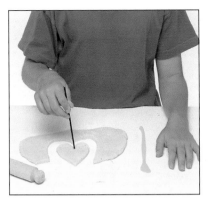

1 Trace the large heart on page 11 to make the template. Roll out a piece of salt dough to about 1 cm thick and cut out the shape using the template. Make a hole at the top of the heart with a garden stick or skewer. Place the heart on a piece of parchment paper on a baking tray and bake it in the oven for about five hours at 120°C/ 250°F/Gas ½.

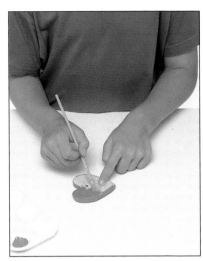

2 When the heart has cooled, gently smooth any rough edges with a piece of sandpaper. You can then paint the heart.

3 Once the paint has dried, glue on some sequins, gemstones and glitter to match or contrast with the paint.

4 Thread a piece of coloured cord or ribbon through the hole and tie the two ends in a knot to fit around your neck.

Heart Bracelet

Dress up for a party and wear this fun bracelet. You could make other bracelets with stars or flowers.

YOU WILL NEED

Salt dough
Rolling pin
Biscuit cutter
Parchment paper
Baking tray
Oven gloves
Cooling rack
Sandpaper
Acrylic paint
Paintbrush
Varnish
Coloured card
Scissors
Glue

1 Roll out a piece of salt dough to about 1 cm thick. It must be big enough for you to cut out five hearts from it.

2 Using a heart-shaped biscuit cutter, cut out five hearts for each bracelet. Place the hearts on a piece of parchment paper on a baking tray and bake them in the oven for about four hours at 120°C/250°F/Gas ½.

3 When they have cooled, smooth down the edges with a piece of sandpaper. Paint the hearts in lots of bright colours, varnish them and leave them to dry.

4 Cut a band of coloured card wide enough to fit the hearts onto and long enough to fit round your wrist, with a bit overlapping. Glue the two ends together.

5 Glue the hearts onto the card. Hold each one in place until the glue has set a bit before sticking the next one on.

51

Place Name Boats

Jazz up your birthday party table with one of these boats at each place setting. This way no one will squabble over where to sit!

YOU WILL NEED

Salt dough
Rolling pin
Ruler
Knife
Garden sticks
Parchment paper
Baking tray
Oven gloves
Cooling rack
Sandpaper
Acrylic paint
Paintbrush
Varnish
Coloured paper
Glue

1 Roll out a piece of salt dough to about 2 cm thick. Cut out the base of the boat to measure 8 cm wide. Shape one end of the base into a gentle point.

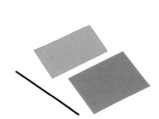

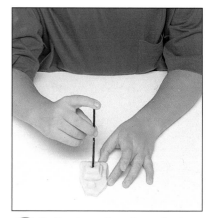

2 Roll out another piece of salt dough to approximately 1 cm thick. Cut out two squares of salt dough, one smaller than the other, to make the cabin of the boat, then stick them onto the base with a dab of water. Cut a garden stick into a 6-cm length and with it make a hole through the boat from the top of the cabin. Make several boats in the same way. Place them on a piece of parchment paper on a baking tray and bake them for about five hours at 120°C/250°F/Gas ½.

3 When the boats have hardened, remove them from the oven with a pair of oven gloves and place them on a cooling rack. When they have cooled, smooth the edges with a piece of sandpaper, then paint and varnish them.

4 Paint the garden sticks and glue one into each hole. Cut triangles of coloured paper and write friends' names on them. Finally glue one to the top of each stick.

Ice Cream Fridge Magnets

These magnets look so tasty you could almost eat them! They will liven up any fridge door.

YOU WILL NEED

Salt dough
Rolling pin
Knife
Parchment paper
Baking tray
Oven gloves
Cooling rack
Sandpaper
Acrylic paint
Paintbrush
Varnish
Magnet pieces
Glue

1 Trace the ice cream on page 11 to make the template. Roll out a piece of salt dough to 1 cm thick. Place the template on the dough and cut out two ice cream shapes.

2 Place the ice creams on a piece of parchment paper on a baking tray. Decorate the ice cream cones with the blade of a knife to make a criss-cross pattern on each one. Bake for about four hours at 120°C/250°F/Gas ½.

3 When the ice creams have hardened, remove the baking tray from the oven. After the shapes have cooled, smooth the edges with a piece of sandpaper. Paint the ice creams in delicious colours and apply a coat of varnish.

4 Glue a magnet piece onto the back of each ice cream and leave the glue to harden before sticking the ice creams onto the fridge door.

Stringy Pot

Believe it or not, it is not difficult to make a salt dough bowl; all you need is an ovenproof bowl as the mould. This bowl had string wrapped around it before it went into the oven which made an interesting pattern.

YOU WILL NEED

Salt dough   Cooling rack
Rolling pin   Oven gloves
Ovenproof bowl   Sandpaper
Vegetable oil   Acrylic paint
Knife   Paintbrush
String   Varnish

1 Roll out a piece of salt dough to approximately 1.5 cm thick and large enough to cover the bowl easily. Rub oil over the outside of the bowl and gently lay the salt dough over the bowl, smoothing it into place.

2 Trim away the excess dough around the rim of the bowl with a knife, making sure you cut it at the same height all the way round.

3 Starting at the base of the bowl, coil the string around the bowl, gently pressing it into place. Put it in the oven to bake for about six hours at 120°C/250°F/Gas $\frac{1}{2}$.

4 When the bowl has cooled, gently remove the ovenproof bowl and smooth the salt dough with a piece of sandpaper. Paint the bowl and finish off with a coat of varnish.

actus

The good thing about *this* cactus is that you won't prick yourself! Make your own collection of cacti in different shapes and sizes.

YOU WILL NEED

Salt dough

Garden stick

Parchment paper

Baking tray

Oven gloves

Cooling rack

Sandpaper

Acrylic paint

Paintbrush

Sequins

Glitter glue

Mini flowerpot

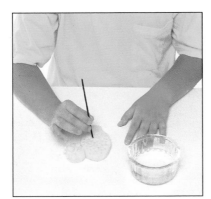

2 Mould a piece of salt dough for the top lobe of the cactus and stick it onto the main cactus with a dab of water and a piece of wet salt dough. Decorate the cactus with spots using the end of a garden stick. Place the cactus on a piece of parchment paper on a baking tray and bake it in the oven for about five hours at 120°C/250°F/Gas ½.

1 Mould the main body of the cactus. Make sure that the base will fit into a mini flowerpot.

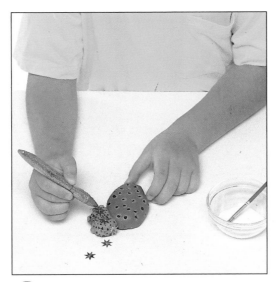

3 Remove from the oven, and leave to cool on a cooling rack. Smooth off any rough edges with sandpaper. Paint the cactus green and leave the paint to dry.

4 Decorate the top lobe of the cactus with sequins and glitter glue and place the cactus in a mini flowerpot. It should just sit in it quite neatly.

59

Bowl with **F**eet

This bowl is useful for odds and ends. It would also make a lovely present and could be filled with sweets.

YOU WILL NEED

Salt dough
Rolling pin
Ovenproof bowl
Vegetable oil
Knife
Baking tray
Cooling rack
Oven gloves
Sandpaper
Acrylic paint
Paintbrush
Varnish

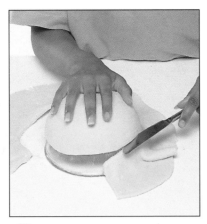

1 Roll out a piece of salt dough to about 1.5 cm thick and large enough to cover the bowl. Rub oil over the outside of the bowl and gently lay the dough over the bowl, smoothing it into place.

2 Trim away the excess dough around the rim of the bowl with a knife, making sure that the edge is level all the way round.

3 Roll four small balls of salt dough the same size and stick them to the base of the bowl with a dab of water and a piece of sticky dough. Place the whole thing on a baking tray and put it in the oven to bake for about six hours at 120°C/250°F/Gas ½.

4 When the bowl has hardened remove it from the oven with a pair of oven gloves and place it on a cooling rack. When the bowl and the salt dough have cooled, gently remove the ovenproof bowl and smooth the edges of the salt dough bowl with a piece of sandpaper. Paint the bowl and add a coat of varnish.

Spotty **C**lock

Watch time tick by
on this spotty clock.

YOU WILL NEED

Salt dough
Rolling pin
Plate
Knife
Garden stick
Clock hands and
  workings
Round pastry cutter

Parchment paper
Baking tray
Oven gloves
Cooling rack
Sandpaper
Acrylic paint
Paintbrush
Varnish

1 Roll out a piece of salt dough to approximately 1 cm thick. Place a plate on the dough and cut round it. Find the centre of the clock and make a hole with a garden stick. Make sure the clock workings will go through this hole.

2 Roll out another piece of salt dough to about 5 mm thick and cut out rounds of dough with the round pastry cutter. Stick four rounds of dough onto the clock base with a dab of water to mark 12, 3, 6 and 9 and stick the other rounds randomly around these points. Bake the clock on a piece of parchment paper on a baking tray for about five hours at 120°C/250°F/Gas ½.

3 When the clock has cooled, smooth the edges with a piece of sandpaper. Paint the background in a light colour. Paint the edge and rounds in contrasting colours. Use the same colour for the four rounds for 12, 3, 6 and 9.

4 Mark the four points of the clock face by painting on the numbers. When the paint has dried, apply a coat of varnish. Attach the clock hands and workings through the hole in the centre.

ACKNOWLEDGEMENTS

The Publishers would like to thank the following children for modelling for this book, and their parents for making it possible for them to do so:

Gurjit Kaur Bilkhu
Vikramjit Singh Bilkhu
Kirsty Fraser
Rean Johnson
Alex Lindblom-Smith
Sophie Lindblom-Smith
Tania Murphy
Kim Peterson.